Black Girl's Dollars and Dreams.

A step-by-step practical guide to Money Mastery, gaining Financial Freedom and living your dreams.

Bonus:30-Days Money Makeover Challenge: Simple Steps to Financial Freedom

By
Mary S. Craver

Disclaimer:

The information provided in this book is for general informational purposes only. The author and publisher assume no responsibility for errors, inaccuracies, or omissions, and expressly disclaim any liability for any loss or damage incurred by any person due to the use or reliance on any information in this book. While every effort has been made to provide accurate and up-to-date information, the rapidly changing nature of personal development and time management means that the content may not always reflect the most current research or trends. This book is not intended to replace expert advice.

Readers are encouraged to seek professional guidance for their specific circumstances. The author and publisher disclaim any responsibility for actions taken by readers based on the information provided in this book. Any product or company names mentioned in this book are for identification purposes only and do not constitute an endorsement or recommendation. The views expressed by the author are solely their own and do not necessarily reflect the views of any affiliated organizations or individuals.

About the Author

 Meet the smart author of "Black Girl's Dollars and Dreams,". Mary S. Craver is a passionate advocate for financial freedom who offers the world of finance a unique blend of competence, relatability, and humour.

Mary S. Craver takes you on a trip that goes beyond typical financial guidance, drawing on personal experiences and a deep grasp of the issues encountered by the Black community. Mary S. Craver gives a fresh perspective with a background in Banking and Finance, making complex concepts simple and empowering. Mary S. Craver is more than simply a writer; she is a guide who is dedicated to changing the financial narrative for Black females and beyond. Prepare to be inspired, enlightened, and empowered by the insights and wisdom offered by this revolutionary guide.

Join her on this financial emancipation journey, where expertise meets relatability and empowerment becomes a reality. Your financial transformation begins with the advice of a competent change agent. Prepare to be inspired, informed, and empowered by Mary S. Craver's wisdom and insights provided in this revolutionary handbook.

Table of contents:

Introduction:

Defining Richness

In the goal of financial independence, the concept of wealth goes beyond monetary value. This introduction digs into the varied nature of wealth, investigating its subjective connotations and ramifications for the Black girl's financial empowerment path. It lays the groundwork for a thorough examination of wealth that includes not only financial abundance but also personal fulfilment, cultural identity, and the empowerment of future generations.

In a world where financial success is frequently defined narrowly, this introduction challenges conventional assumptions by posing a fundamental question: What does richness genuinely mean to you as a Black female navigating the complex landscape of financial freedom?

We set out on a voyage beyond the bounds of traditional prosperity, discovering the riches found in cultural heritage, personal development, and community. This exploration complements the search for financial well-being by recognising that true wealth consists of a tapestry of experiences, knowledge, and self-discovery.

As we read through this guide, we ask you to consider your beliefs, goals, and personal definitions of success. By redefining richness, we hope to empower you to create a financial narrative that reflects your uniqueness while also contributing to the collective wealth of the Black community. Join us on this journey as we uncover the levels of riches that go far beyond monetary value.

Examples of how people define wealth.

1. Relationships that are fulfilling:

For some, the quality of their relationships—family, friends, and meaningful connections that bring joy and support—defines their wealth.

Individuals may find richness in constant self-improvement, learning new talents, and gaining knowledge that enriches their lives.

Many people regard good health as true wealth, viewing physical and mental well-being as the cornerstone of a rich and meaningful life.

2. **Cultural Identity and Heritage**: For some, wealth is associated with conserving and celebrating one's cultural identity, embracing traditions, and passing them down to future generations.

Richness can be characterised as a collection of events, adventures, and memories that contribute to a well-lived life.

3. **Contributions to Others:** Some people define wealth as the ability to make a good difference in the lives of others, whether via acts of kindness, mentorship, or generosity.

4. **Work-Life Balance**: Achieving a harmonic balance between work and personal life is regarded as a type of wealth, giving time to pursue interests and enjoy leisure.
5. **Spiritual Fulfilment:** For many people, wealth is associated with spiritual or philosophical ideas that provide meaning and purpose beyond the material aspects of life.

6..Ability and Autonomy: For some people, having the ability to make choices, follow goals, and live life on their terms is a defining component of wealth.

7. Connection with Nature: Whether through outdoor activities or a sense of environmental stewardship, appreciating and connecting with nature can add to one's idea of richness.

Chapter One:

Your Relationship with Wealth.

Money is more than simply bills and coins to me. It's like having a helpful friend who can make your life easier. Knowing how to use money wisely is like having a superpower, I've discovered.

Growing up, I realised that having enough money is vital, but knowing how to make it work for me is even more important. It's not just about saving for a rainy day (though that is vital), but also about using money to improve my life and the lives of those around me.

Money, to me, is a trip rather than a possession. It's about creating objectives, conquering challenges, and celebrating my success. Money isn't simply about having a lot of it; it's about having enough of it. It's about putting it to good use to benefit my community and make the world a better place.

So my financial story is like an adventure. It's not just about the numbers; it's about developing as a person, keeping loyal to myself, and creating positive changes for myself and others. Understanding how you view and manage money in your life is necessary for defining your relationship with it. It's similar to describing your relationship with a beneficial buddy. Here's an easy way to put it:

Consider money to be a friend. How do you treat this acquaintance? Do you save money for future adventures? Do you make preparations to assist one another when necessary? That is your relationship with money—how you handle it, save it, spend it, and use it to improve your life and the lives of people around you. It is about setting objectives, confronting problems, and ensuring that your money supports your path and the things that are important to you.

Chapter Two:

The Black Girl's Perspective on Financial Freedom.

The Black girl's viewpoint on financial freedom is reminiscent of a tremendous story of fortitude and achievement. It is about tackling difficult difficulties and transforming them into stepping stones. Her quest, for financial freedom is about more than simply gaining money; it's about empowering not only herself but her entire community.

Consider education to be a significant character in this drama. Not only is school knowledge important, but so is learning about money, starting businesses, and making wise decisions. It's a means for a Black girl to negotiate the financial world and generate possibilities for herself and others.

Cultural identity is also an important aspect of this story. It's about appreciating her roots and using her financial status to better her community. Wealth is viewed negatively by the Black girl. The Black girl views riches as an instrument for positive change, not just for her benefit, but for the benefit of all.

Financial freedom, in her opinion, is more than just personal accomplishments. It is about starting enterprises, allowing others to succeed, and leaving a legacy of power and growth. The story of a Black girl's road to financial freedom is one of empowerment, changing the narrative for herself and future generations.

Chapter Three:

Understanding Conscious Spending

Recognising Conscious Spending

Conscious spending is similar to having an in-depth conversation with your money. It's not just about how much money you have or where you spend it; it's about being deliberate and conscious of the financial decisions you make.

Consider it being aware of where your money is going and how it connects with your values and aspirations. It isn't only about purchasing things; it is also about investing in experiences, relationships, and the things that mean to you.

When you spend consciously, you make decisions that reflect your priorities. It comes down to asking yourself, "Does this purchase add value to my life?" Does it add to my well-being or assist me in attaining my goals?" It's a bit like curating your spending habits to design a life that reflects your values.

This method also entails being conscious of the influence of your spending on the world around you. Whether it's supporting businesses that share your beliefs or making decisions that decrease your environmental imprint, conscientious spending goes beyond personal advantages to assist the larger society. Understanding conscious spending is essentially about making your money work for you in a way that reflects who you are and what you stand for. It's not just about the numbers; it's about crafting a financial narrative that aligns with your values and adds to a more fulfilling existence. Spending deliberately entails making deliberate decisions to fit your purchases with your values and financial goals. Here are some practical strategies to help you spend more wisely:

1. **Establish Your Values and Priorities:**
   - Determine what is most important to you in life.
   - Determine your short- and long-term financial objectives.

2. Make a Budget:
- Make a list of your monthly income and spending.
- Distribute monies to categories that reflect your values and priorities.

3. Keep Track of Your Spending:
- Keep track of your spending. Monitor your spending with budgeting applications or tools.

4. Put needs ahead of wants:
- Distinguish between necessary necessities and luxuries.
- Before making non-essential purchases, be sure your necessities are fulfilled.

5. Avoid Making Impulse Purchases:
- Consider the necessity of a purchase before making one.
- To reduce impulse purchases, wait 24 hours before purchasing non-urgent things.

6. Before You Buy, Do Your Homework:
- Examine the companies and brands that you support.
- Select items and services that adhere to ethical and sustainable principles.
- Local and sustainable enterprises should be prioritised to contribute to your community.
- Select products with a low environmental impact.

7. Set Spending limitations:
- Set spending limitations for discretionary categories.
- To avoid overspending, stick to these spending limitations.

Mindful Spending entails being present and attentive when making purchases.

Think about the long-term value and influence of your spending decisions.

Review and adjust your spending habits regularly.

As your values and ambitions change, so should your budget and priorities.

By implementing these practices into your daily life, you may develop the habit of conscious spending, ensuring that your money decisions reflect your beliefs and contribute positively to your well-being and the environment around you.

Chapter Four:

Navigating Cultural Influences on Finances.

Understanding the rhythm and melody of your financial tale is similar to navigating cultural influences on finances. Recognising that your background influences how you relate to money and the decisions you make. Let's dissect it:

1. **Money and Cultural Values:**
- Consider the importance of money in your culture.
- Is it more concerned with saving, investing, or sustaining a family?

- .Consider how family expectations influence your financial decisions.
- Is your approach to providing for family members influenced by cultural norms?

2. Celebrations and Financial Planning:
- What is your culture's attitude towards celebrations and their financial implications?
- It is critical to strike a balance between cultural traditions and financial responsibility.

3. Influence Across Generations:
- Consider how the financial practices of your family have been passed down over generations.
- Determine which practices you wish to keep or change.

4. Cultural Attitudes Towards Debt:
- Investigate your culture's attitude towards borrowing and debt.
- It is critical to strike a balance between cultural expectations and sound financial procedures.

5. **Community solidarity:** During times of financial difficulty, many cultures emphasise collective solidarity.
- Investigate how your cultural community might be a resource at difficult times.

6. **Education and job Options**:
- Think about how cultural norms influence your educational and job choices.
- It is critical to strike a balance between cultural ideals and personal goals.

7. Investing in Cultural Experiential Learning:
- Cultural effects frequently extend beyond cash to include experiences.
- Budgeting for cultural events and travel may be necessary.
- Budgeting While Respecting Traditions:

- It is critical to strike a balance between honouring cultural traditions and maintaining under budget.
- It's about finding ways to rejoice without jeopardising one's financial security.

8. Open Communication:

- Talk about money openly with your family and community.
- Understanding cultural impacts enables improved collaboration and the achievement of common financial goals.

Recognising the wonderful details that create your financial journey is the key to navigating cultural influences on finances. It's a dance between tradition and modernity, ensuring that your cultural heritage enriches rather than limits your financial decisions.

Chapter Five:

Building Financial Awareness.

Building financial awareness is like turning on the lights in a room; it is about casting light on your financial landscape, understanding where your money flows, and making informed decisions. Let's go into the specifics:

1. **Keep Track of Your Spending:**
- Begin by keeping track of your daily expenses.
- Categorise spending to uncover patterns and areas for improvement.

2. **Make a Budget:**
- Create a budget that is in line with your income and financial goals.
- Distribute monies to necessary categories such as bills, savings, and discretionary expenditures.

3. **Examine your bank statements:**
- Check your bank statements regularly to comprehend inflows and outflows.
- Determine any extraneous fees or inconsistencies.

4. **Examining Credit Reports:**
- Obtain your credit report once a year.
- Examine it for accuracy and address any discrepancies as soon as possible.

5. **Set financial objectives:**
- Define your short-term and long-term financial goals.
- Having specific goals, whether for a trip or an emergency fund, provides direction.

6. **Planning for an Emergency Fund:**
- Create an emergency fund to cover unexpected expenses.
- As a financial safety net, aim for three to six months' worth of living expenditures.

7. Understand Your Income:
- Determine your monthly after-tax income.
- Consider other income streams or growth options.
- Consider Subscription Services:
- Examine memberships and recurring subscriptions.
- Cancel any services that aren't adding any value.

8. Comparison Shopping:
- Before making large purchases, do your homework and compare prices.
- Utilise discounts, promotions, and loyalty programmes.
- Learn about many investment alternatives through investment education.
- Understand each investment's risks and potential returns.

9. Keep Up With Financial News:
- Keep up with economic trends and financial news.
- Recognise how external circumstances may affect your financial condition.

10. Financial check-ins regularly:
- Plan regular reviews of your financial situation.
- As your life circumstances change, adjust your budget and goals.

11. Seek Professional Advice:
- Talk to financial advisors about your options.
- They can provide tailored advice based on your specific financial position.

Building financial awareness entails making a series of deliberate efforts to explore the complexities of your financial world. It's all about being proactive, remaining informed, and always modifying your approach as you go along your financial path.

Chapter Six:

Developing Healthy Money Habits.

Creating healthy money habits entails incorporating financial mindfulness into your everyday routine. It is a continuous process of self-reflection, education, and proactive decision-making that creates the groundwork for a prosperous and secure financial future.

Creating a habit is a gradual process that requires incorporating behaviour into your daily routine. Here's a step-by-step strategy for forming long-lasting habits:

1. **Start Small:**
- Begin by implementing a small, manageable version of the desired behaviour.
- Smaller actions are more easily integrated into your everyday routine.

2. Set precise and Achievable Goals:
- Define precise and attainable goals for your behaviour.
- To keep oneself motivated, clearly define what success looks like.

3. Create a Trigger:
- Connect your new habit to an existing routine or a particular trigger.
- This helps to anchor the behaviour to a regular part of your day.

4. Maintain Consistency:
- To reinforce the habit, aim for everyday repetition.

- Consistency is essential for the formation of strong neuronal connections.

5. Monitor Your Progress:
- Monitor your daily efforts with a habit tracker or journal.
- Visualising your progress might help you stay motivated and reinforce the habit loop.

6. Maintain Accountability:
- Tell a friend or family member about your habit-building adventure.
- Having someone to motivate and hold you accountable increases commitment.

7. Celebrate tiny Victories:
- Recognise and celebrate your accomplishments, no matter how tiny.
- The habit loop is strengthened by positive reinforcement.

8. Learn from Failures:
- Consider missed days or problems as learning opportunities.
- Determine what caused the setback and modify your strategy accordingly.

9. Make It Interesting:
- Look for ways to make the habit more fun or rewarding.
- Positive associations make habit formation more likely.

10. Be Patient:
- It takes time for habits to establish, so be patient with yourself.
- Avoid drastic adjustments and instead concentrate on steady gains.

11. Make Use of Reminders:
- Set reminders on your phone or place visual cues around you.
- Gentle reminders assist in reinforcing the behaviour until it becomes automatic.

12. Pair with Existing Habits:
- Connect the new habit to one that already exists.
- This helps to integrate the new behaviour into an existing routine.

13. Adjust as Needed:
- If the habit isn't sticking, be willing to change your strategy.
- Experiment with different triggers, timeframes, and behaviour modifications.

14. Reflect regularly:
- Take some time to ponder your habit-building journey.
- Evaluate the influence on your life and alter your goals accordingly.

15. Make a Minimum Commitment:
- Commit to a bare-bones version of the habit on days when motivation is low.
  This ensures that the behaviour remains consistent.
- Remember that habit formation is a process that requires repetition, positive reinforcement, and adaptability.

By implementing these tactics into your everyday routine, you boost your chances of effectively adapting a new behaviour into your daily life.

Creating healthy money habits is similar to planting a garden; it takes time, attention, and constant effort. Let's go into the specifics of developing these behaviours for a financially prosperous future:

1. Create a Budget:

Creating a budget is an essential step in efficiently managing your finances. Here's a step-by-step guide to creating a practical and realistic budget:

- ***Compile Financial Information:***

Gather information about your earnings, such as your salary, bonuses, and any additional sources of revenue.

- ***Make a list of your expenses:***

Determine and classify your normal monthly expenses.

Rent or mortgage, utilities, groceries, transportation, insurance, debt payments, and discretionary spending are examples of categories.

- ***Differentiate Fixed and Variable Expenses:***

Distinguish between fixed expenses (such as rent) and variable expenses (such as entertainment or dining out).

- ***Set financial objectives:***

Set short-term and long-term financial objectives.

These objectives will help guide your budget and prioritise your expenditures.

- ***Determine Your Monthly Income:***

Total your monthly income by adding together all sources of income.

- ***Divide your income by your expenses:***

Prioritise critical spending with your cash.

Make housing, electricity, groceries, and loan payments your top priorities.

- ***Make a Savings item:***

    Include a savings item in your budget.

Save a portion of your salary for emergency cash, long-term goals, or retirement.

- ***Consider Irregular Expenses:***

 Include one-time or annual expenses (such as insurance payments, vacations, or presents).

Divide these expenses by 12 to incorporate them into your monthly budget.

- ***Make use of a budgeting tool or a spreadsheet:***

To organise and track your spending, use budgeting tools, software, or a basic spreadsheet.

Technology can help to speed up the process and provide insights into your purchasing habits.

- ***Examine and revise:***

Review your budget regularly to verify it is in line with your financial objectives.

Make necessary adjustments to account for changes in income or expenses.

Prioritise the creation of an emergency fund to cover unforeseen expenses.

Budget for three to six months of living expenditures.

- ***Debt Repayment:***

   If you have outstanding obligations, set aside some money in your budget to pay them off. Prioritise high-interest bills first.

- ***Be practical:***

Set reasonable budget expectations.

To establish a reasonable and attainable plan, be honest about your spending patterns.

- ***Involve Family or Housemates:***

   If possible, include family or housemates in the budgeting process.

Collaborate on common spending and financial objectives.

- ***Regularly monitor and adjust:***

Maintain a tight eye on your real spending in comparison to your budget.

To stay on track, adjust categories or allocations as needed.

Budgeting is a continuous process of fine-tuning and adapting to your financial circumstances. By following these steps, you can create a budget that is in line with your objectives and gives a clear plan for managing your finances.

2. Prioritise Wants vs. Needs:

Understanding the distinction between wants and necessities is essential for making wise financial decisions. Here's an explanation for each:

Needs:

- *Survival Requirements*: The basic ingredients required for human survival are needs. Food, drink, shelter, and clothing are examples of necessities. Meeting these requirements assures physical health.
- *Needs are non-negotiable;* they are required to maintain a minimal standard of living. You must, for example, have a place to live and enough food to support yourself.
- *Needs are, in general,* universal. While precise requirements may differ, human core needs remain universal across cultures and societies.
- *Priority*: Meeting needs come before wants. When dealing with limited finances, the first focus should be to ensure that your necessities are addressed.

Wants:

- *Preferences and Desires:* Wants are objects or experiences that are desired but not necessary for survival. Luxury things, entertainment, vacations, and non-essential gadgets are examples.
- *Subjective*: Wants are highly subjective and can differ greatly from person to person. What one person considers a luxury may be considered a need by another.

Wants are not generally required for a basic level of living, in contrast to needs. Individual interests, preferences, and cultural variables frequently impact them.

- *Can Change Over Time:* Trends, preferences, and individual circumstances all influence wants. Personal priorities and lifestyles can cause them to shift over time.

Balancing Needs and Desires:

- *Prioritisation*: It is critical to prioritise requirements above wants while managing your budget. Before dedicating resources to discretionary spending, ensure that your necessities are satisfied.

- ***Budgeting***: Creating a budget allows you to purposefully allocate finances to both needs and wants. It enables you to budget for discretionary expenditures without sacrificing critical needs.
- ***Mindful Spending***: Mindful spending entails being aware of the distinction between needs and wants. Examine your purchases regularly to verify they are in line with your priorities and financial goals.

In summary, requirements are products or experiences that are desirable but not necessary for survival and maintaining a basic level of life, whereas desires are items or experiences that are desirable but not necessary. Balancing the fulfilment of both necessities and desires is critical to financial well-being.

3. Building an Emergency Fund:

Set aside a portion of your income to create an emergency fund. Put three to six months' worth of living expenses away. Set up automatic transfers to a savings account to save time.

This guarantees that savings are consistent without relying simply on willpower.

4. Debt Management:

Pay off high-interest obligations first.
Create a repayment strategy to strategically reduce outstanding obligations.

5. Become Financially Informed:

Make time to study about personal money.
Understand investment, compound interest, and the significance of credit scores.
Establish short-term and long-term financial goals and review them regularly.
Review and revise your goals regularly to reflect changes in your life.

6. Practice Delayed gratification:

Put off non-essential purchases. Delaying gratification can help you control your impulse spending.

7. Shop and bargain wisely:

Negotiate your costs and look for better bargains on services.
Practice conscious purchasing by comparing costs and looking for bargains.

8. Keep Track of Your Credit Score:

Maintain a record of your credit score. A good credit score opens the door to more lucrative financial opportunities.

9. Diversify Income Streams:

Look for extra sources of income.
This can include side jobs, freelance work, or passive income.

10. Assess Financial Health regularly:

Perform periodic financial health checks.
Examine your net worth, investment performance, and tactics as needed.

11. Create a Retirement Plan:

Make monthly contributions to your retirement account.
Utilise employer-sponsored programmes and contact a financial expert for long-term planning.

12. Open Communication:

Talk about your financial goals and practices with your family or partners.
Encourage transparency to collaborate towards common goals.

13. Celebrate Financial Achievements:
Recognise and appreciate accomplishments along the way.
Recognising success, whether it's paying off a debt or attaining a financial goal, encourages beneficial habits.

Chapter Seven:

Setting Financial Goals and Milestones.

Goal Setting and Milestone Achievement

Setting financial goals is similar to creating a road map for a long journey. It entails visualising where you want to go, breaking down goals into manageable steps, and celebrating minor victories along the route. This essay delves into the complexities of creating financial objectives and milestones, providing insights into the deliberate process of charting one's financial trajectory.

1. Values and Priorities Analysis:

A profound examination of personal beliefs and priorities is at the heart of developing financial goals. The compass that guides the trip is understanding what is important. It entails weighing short-term desires against long-term goals and laying the groundwork for significant financial goals.

2. Clarity through Specificity:

To effectively navigate the financial roadmap, goals must be specific. Vague ideas like "save money" become concrete goals like "save $1,000 in six months. This function provides both clarity and a definite endpoint on the financial journey.

3. Goals Classification for a Comprehensive Approach:

Goals might range from current necessities to distant ambitions. A structured method is provided by categorising them into short-term, medium-term, and long-term objectives. Each category necessitates separate preparation and consideration to ensure a well-rounded financial strategy.

4. Assigning Timeframes and Measuring Success:
Giving goals realistic timetables gives a sense of urgency and accountability. Measuring success becomes more concrete, moving from ideals to real accomplishments. A quantifiable objective could be to save a certain amount of money each month or to pay off a credit card by a certain date.

5. Financial Assessment:
Before charting a course, it is critical to do a complete assessment of the present financial picture. A reasonable beginning point is to assess income, expenses, debts, and savings. It's like learning the topography before heading into unfamiliar territory.

6. Prioritisation and Importance Order:
Not all objectives are equally important or urgent. Prioritisation entails choosing which goals require immediate attention and which may be pursued over time. This stage guarantees that efforts are focused on the most important financial requirements.

7. Actionable Stages and Milestone Breakdown:
Making goals a reality necessitates breaking them down into actionable stages. Each step becomes a marker of progress, a milestone. Saving $100 per month, for example, becomes a tangible milestone towards a greater savings goal.

8. Celebrating Achievements:
The financial journey is about more than just getting to the end goal; it is also about enjoying the journey itself. Celebrating accomplishments, no matter how minor, increases drive. It turns the financial journey into a series of pleasurable moments, making the effort worthwhile.
The financial roadmap must be reviewed and adjusted regularly. Regular evaluations are required to adjust goals to changing circumstances. Life changes, priorities move, and financial circumstances shift. Changing the course ensures that it remains relevant and effective.

9. Collaboration and Seeking Guidance:
Starting a financial journey does not imply going it alone. Seeking financial guidance or involving family members promotes collaboration. It turns a single journey into a group experience, forming a support network for mutual success.

10. Staying Inspired:
The path might be difficult, but staying inspired is critical. Revisiting the reasons for each goal, visualising the good impact of accomplishments, and remaining optimistic about the possibilities keep the spirit high throughout the financial journey.

Finally, defining financial objectives is a time-consuming but rewarding exercise. It necessitates reflection, strategic planning, and dedication to the path. The financial trip, like any expedition, is formed not only by the destinations reached but also by the experiences gained along the way. It is a path of personal development, resilience, and financial well-being.

Chapter Eight:

Investing in Yourself – Education and Skills.

Investing in oneself via education and skill development is a life-changing commitment to personal and professional development. It requires devoting time, effort, and resources to expanding your knowledge, learning new abilities, and evolving continuously. Here's a closer look at investing in yourself through education and skills:

Continuous Education:

- **Education as a Lifelong Process:** When education is viewed as a lifelong journey, it indicates a continual commitment to learning. It extends beyond formal education to include lifelong self-directed learning and skill acquisition.

- **Formal education includes degrees and certifications**. Obtaining formal education, such as degrees or certifications, is a real method to invest in oneself. It brings up new opportunities and broadens your knowledge base.

- **Developing Skills**: Adapting to Change: Acquiring new skills is critical for adaptation in a continuously changing world. Investing in skill development keeps you relevant and competitive in your chosen sector.

- **Personal Development**: Beyond Professional Skills: Investing in yourself is about more than just your professional talents. Personal development is also involved, as is the nurturing of skills such as resilience, emotional intelligence, and effective communication.

- **Entrepreneurial Ventures:** Laying the Groundwork: Investing in education and skills is essential for ambitious businesses. It provides people with the knowledge and skills they need to handle the hurdles of beginning and maintaining a business.
- **Increased self-assurance:**

Ability self-assurance: Education and skill development help to boost confidence. As you gain information and acquire new talents, your confidence in your abilities improves, which benefits both your personal and professional life.

- **Networking and Collaboration:** Meeting Like-Minded People: Educational pursuits frequently provide opportunities to network and collaborate with others who share similar interests. These connections can lead to beneficial collaborations, mentorships, and shared learning opportunities.

- **Staying Ahead of Trends:** Adaptability to Industry Changes: Investing in education guarantees that you stay ahead of trends. Professionals who want to flourish in changing circumstances must be adaptable.

- **Meaning and fulfilment:**

Alignment with Passion: Investing in education and skills that align with your passions helps you feel fulfilled and purposeful. It elevates learning from a necessary evil to a source of delight and personal fulfilment.

- **Financial Gains:**

Long-Term Financial Gains: While the immediate expenses of education and skill development are obvious, the long-term financial advantages are frequently significant. Common effects include increased income potential and job promotion.

- **Embracing Challenges:**

Meeting Challenges Head-On: Education and skills enable people to meet challenges head-on. Instead of being overwhelmed by new situations, you gain confidence in dealing with them, promoting a development mentality.

- **Life Balance:**
  Holistic Development: Investing in oneself entails holistic development. A well-rounded and meaningful existence is ensured by balancing career and personal progress.

Investing in oneself through education and skills is, in essence, a great strategy for personal and professional growth. It is a commitment to lifelong learning and progress, as well as to constant improvement and flexibility.

○ 8.1 Identifying Marketable Skills.

Identifying marketable abilities is an important step in navigating today's employment market and achieving professional success. In a world where sectors change quickly, having in-demand talents might help you stand out. Here's a look at the process of determining marketable skills:

- **Self-Awareness**:
Recognising Your Strengths: Begin by evaluating your strengths and limitations. Reflect on your professional and personal experiences to find areas where you thrive.

- **Industry Research: Stay Current on Industry Trends**:
  Keep up with industry changes and technological advances. Identify developing abilities that are becoming increasingly important in your sector.

- **Job Market Evaluation:**
Examine Job Descriptions: Examine job descriptions for positions that you want or are interested in. Determine the most prevalent skills that employers are looking for.

- **Connect with Professionals Through Networking:**
Networking with professionals in your field might provide useful information. Learn about the skills that have aided their success and inquire about the skills that are now in demand.

- **Online Job Platforms**:
  Investigate Online Job Platforms: LinkedIn and industry-specific job boards frequently emphasise the abilities that employers are actively seeking. Examine job postings for recurring skill requirements.

- **Research Training and Development Programmes**:
  Investigate professional development programmes, workshops, or courses that meet current skill needs. Courses are available on online platforms.

- **Versatility and adaptability:**
  Develop Adaptable Skills: Highlight abilities that demonstrate your versatility. The capacity to learn new technologies and adapt to changing situations is highly rewarded in a dynamic job environment.

- **Soft abilities:**
  Understand the Importance of Soft Skills: Soft skills such as communication, teamwork, and problem-solving are becoming increasingly important in addition to technical expertise. Employers desire individuals who can effectively contribute to team dynamics.

- **Leadership and Management Capabilities:**
  Develop Your Leadership Skills: Leadership and management abilities can be applied to a variety of positions. These abilities are essential for project management and team leadership.

- **Data Literacy**:
  Understand Data Analytics: Being literate in data analysis is a valuable ability in today's data-driven world. Data tool expertise and the ability to extract insights from large data sets are in high demand.

- **Explore Digital Skills:**
  Digital Marketing and Social Media Management Digital marketing and social media management abilities are in high demand. The ability to use online platforms for marketing objectives can be a useful tool.

- **Language Ability**:

Multilingual abilities: Proficiency in various languages can be a marketable ability in today's globalised environment. It provides options for foreign travel and cross-cultural contact.

- **Cybersecurity Awareness:**

Maintain Your Cybersecurity Knowledge: With the rise of digital dangers, understanding cybersecurity principles and practices is becoming a critical skill in a variety of businesses.

- **Critical Thinking and Problem Solving:**

Develop Analytical Thinking: The capacity to solve complex problems and think critically is highly recognised across the board. Analytical thinking should be highlighted in both your resume and interviews.

- **Credentials and certifications:**

Examine for Industry-Recognized Certifications: Acquire certificates in your field. Employers will notice that you have engaged in learning specific knowledge if you hold industry-recognized certifications.

Identifying marketable abilities requires self-awareness, industry research, and a commitment to continuous growth. You position yourself for success in your career journey by staying tuned in to the changing needs of the job market and proactively gaining in-demand skills.

○ **8.2 Accessing Affordable Education and Training.**

Access to inexpensive education and training is critical to empowering individuals to improve their skills, pursue career objectives, and contribute to personal and societal growth. Here's a look at some ideas and options for making education and training more affordable without breaking the bank:

1. Vocational Schools and Community Colleges:

- ***Programmes at a Low Cost:*** When compared to typical four-year institutions, community colleges and vocational schools frequently provide more economical education and training programmes.

- ***Emphasis on Practical Skills:*** These universities frequently emphasise practical skills essential to specific industries, offering them an affordable option for specialised training.

2. Courses on Online Learning Platforms:

Flexible and Affordable: Courses on online learning platforms are available at a variety of price points.

Many platforms provide free courses or audit possibilities, allowing learners to access educational content without incurring financial costs.

3. Open Educational Resources (OER):

Free Learning Materials: Open Educational Resources (OER) include textbooks, videos, and lecture notes that are freely available online. Platforms online offer free access to high-quality educational resources.

- ***Ideal for Self-Directed Learning:*** OER is especially beneficial for self-directed learners who want to learn at their speed.

3. Programmes Funded by the Government:

- ***Grants and Scholarships:*** Governments frequently provide grants and scholarships to help people pursue education and training.
- ***Employment Training Programmes***: Some governments provide subsidised or free employment training programmes.

4. Employer-Sponsored Training:

On-the-Job Training: Some firms provide on-the-job training programmes, allowing employees to learn new skills without paying extra fees.

- ***Tuition help Programmes***:
Businesses may offer tuition help to employees who are pursuing relevant education or training to improve their abilities.

5. Nonprofit Corporations:

Nonprofit organisations commonly organise efforts to provide affordable education and training, particularly in impoverished communities.

- *Career Development Programmes*: These programmes frequently focus on preparing participants for certain occupations.
- *Grants & Subsidies from the Government:*

Governments may provide targeted financial assistance in the form of grants or subsidies to lessen the financial burden of education and training.

- *Earning-driven Repayment Plans*: Income-driven repayment plans are implemented in several countries, allowing individuals to repay educational debts based on their earning levels.

6. Skill-specialised Bootcamps: rigorous Training Programmes:

Bootcamps provide rigorous training programmes for specialised skills such as coding, digital marketing, and data analytics.

- *Cost-Effective Alternatives:* While certain boot camps may be less expensive than regular education, it is critical to properly explore all possibilities.

7. Initiatives for Local Training:

Community-Based Programmes: Local community organisations and libraries may conduct cost-effective training initiatives that are tailored to the needs of the community.

Participating in local programmes might also provide excellent networking chances for job advancement.

8. Earn-While-Learning Model:

Apprenticeships provide a hands-on approach to learning, allowing individuals to earn a living while learning practical skills.

- *Apprenticeship Programmes:* Many industries, including manufacturing and trades, actively encourage apprenticeship programmes.

9. Payment Installments:

Some educational institutions and training providers provide flexible payment options that allow students to pay for courses in instalments.

- *Deferred Payment opportunities*: Look into opportunities for deferring payment until after the education or training programme is completed.

10. Platforms for Micro-Credentialing:

- *Courses that are both affordable and targeted:* Micro-credentialing platforms such as LinkedIn Learning and Skillshare provide low-cost, brief courses on certain skills or tools.
- *Subscription Models:* Subscription-based platforms offer a wide range of courses for a set monthly charge.

Access to inexpensive education and training is critical for encouraging inclusion and giving opportunities to people from all walks of life. Individuals can learn essential talents without incurring an excessive financial burden by investigating these paths and exploiting available resources.

○ 8.3 Utilizing Online Resources for Skill Development

Using internet resources for skill development has changed the game in the modern era, providing unequalled access to a large array of educational content. Whether you want to learn new technical skills, expand your professional knowledge, or pursue personal hobbies, online tools offer flexibility and convenience. Here's an investigation of how to successfully use these resources for skill development:

- **Platforms for Online Learning:**

Coursera, edX, and Udacity are just a few examples. Courses from prominent universities and institutions are available through platforms such as Coursera, edX, and Udacity. These platforms include a wide range of subjects, allowing students to select courses that are relevant to their objectives.

- **Specialisations and Degrees:**

    Many platforms provide specialised programmes, as well as degree courses, allowing learners to broaden their expertise in specific fields.

Websites that specialise in coding and programming, such as Codecademy and Khan Academy, provide interactive tasks for hands-on learning. Khan Academy offers free instructional content on a wide range of topics.

- ***Duolingo and Babbel:*** Language learning services like Duolingo and Babbel make language acquisition fun and easy, allowing users to learn at their speed.
- ***Tutorials on YouTube:***

A Wide Range of Subjects: YouTube has a variety of tutorials on almost any skill you can think of. There's a tutorial for everything, from photography and graphic design to software development and do-it-yourself projects.

Experts Can Teach You: Many industry experts and professionals offer their expertise on YouTube, providing useful insights and practical advice.

- ***MIT's Open Educational Resources (OER) OpenCourseWare and OpenStax***: Organisations such as MIT and OpenStax provide free and open educational resources such as textbooks, lecture notes, and assignments.

Accessible to All: By making learning resources freely available, OER democratises education and fosters inclusivity.

Learn on the Go with Podcasts and Audiobooks: Podcasts and audiobooks are a great method to learn while on the road. Audible, for example, has a large library of educational information.

- ***Multitasking Learning***: Whether you're commuting or exercising, these materials enable multitasking learning, allowing you to make the most of your time.
- ***Interactive Coding Platforms***: GitHub, HackerRank: Interactive coding platforms such as GitHub and HackerRank allow for hands-on coding experience. GitHub facilitates coding projects, while HackerRank offers coding challenges to help you improve your programming skills.
- ***Community Engagement***: Discussing these issues with the coding community.

Community Engagement: Using these tools to interact with the coding community fosters collaboration and enables learning from real-world projects.

Online Forums and Communities: Stack Overflow, Reddit: Online forums such as Stack Overflow and Reddit provide a venue for asking questions, getting advice, and participating in conversations about various abilities.

Participating in these communities gives networking possibilities and exposes learners to a variety of ideas.

- ***Platforms for Professional Networking***:

LinkedIn Learning provides a variety of courses on professional development, soft skills, and industry-specific expertise.

Networking and Certification: Courses completed on LinkedIn Learning can be displayed on your LinkedIn profile, improving your professional credibility.

Webinars and online workshops:

- ***Opportunities for Live Learning***: Many organisations and educational institutions hold webinars and virtual seminars on specialised areas. These live events allow for discussion and questions.
- ***Keep Up with Trends:*** Attending webinars brings students up to date on industry trends and new technologies.
- ***Online Competitions and Challenges***:

Data science competitions are held on platforms such as Kaggle, while hackathons provide challenges for software engineers. Participating in these events allows you to enhance your practical abilities.

- ***Gamified Learning***: The competitive aspect of challenges and competitions gamifies learning, making it more engaging and dynamic.
- ***Learning Communities on Social Media:***

Twitter Chats and Facebook Groups: Learning communities are hosted by social media platforms via Twitter chats and Facebook groups. These communities offer a forum for debate, resource sharing, and collaboration.

- ***Global Learning Networks***: Connecting with experts all over the world broadens your learning network and exposes you to new perspectives.

Platforms for Micro-Credentialing: Skillshare, LinkedIn Badges: Micro-credentialing platforms such as Skillshare and LinkedIn provide short courses on certain talents. Earning badges or certifications shows future employers your accomplishments.

- ***tailored Learning:*** For people with limited time, these platforms offer tailored, bite-sized learning possibilities.

Udemy and Teachable are two e-learning platforms. E-learning platforms such as Udemy and Teachable feature a plethora of courses created by specialists in various industries. These platforms frequently provide both free and paid courses.

Learners can progress at their own pace, giving them more freedom in managing their schedules.

- ***Tools for Remote Collaboration:***

Zoom and Slack: Remote collaboration solutions such as Zoom and Slack make virtual teamwork possible. Understanding how to use these tools successfully has become a valuable talent, particularly in this day and age of remote access.

Chapter Nine:

Building Multiple Income Streams.

In today's fast-paced world, relying on a single income appears to be a dangerous game. That's where the concept of creating several income streams comes into play, similar to having multiple money faucets operating at the same time. It's not just a financial fad; it's a wise move to strengthen your wallet and prepare it for anything life throws at you.

Consider having multiple jobs, rather than just one, contributing to your bank account. It is not about overwhelming yourself, but rather about providing a safety net. If one source of income fails, you have another to fall back on. This diversification isn't only for financial experts; it's a plan for ordinary people like you and me to ensure our financial security, especially when times are tough. tough.

So, how do you create these many revenue streams? It's a little like sowing various seeds to build a money garden. You may start a side business, work as a freelancer, or sell your services online. The gig economy has made it easier for people to try their hand at various money-making activities, such as driving for Uber or renting out a spare room on Airbnb.

Another aspect of the puzzle is investing. It's similar to putting your money to work for you. Instead of putting all of your money in a bank account, consider investing in stocks, bonds, or even real estate. These investments can generate passive income, such as dividends or rental payments, adding layers to your financial picture. Then there's the whole online money-making world. Do you have a special interest or skill? You may transform that into content (blogs, podcasts, videos) and monetize it through advertisements or sponsorships. It's similar to turning your interests into a source of income. The digital age has created a whole new world of economic opportunities.

But, let's be honest: balancing various revenue streams isn't always a bed of roses. It requires a lot of balancing. You'll need to learn how to manage your time, handle the challenges of being your boss, and perhaps even dabble in investing. It's a voyage that requires preparation and thought.

At the end of the day, developing numerous revenue sources is about having a more adaptive and secure financial existence. It's like having a safety net that allows you to take risks, try new things, and not be concerned about financial setbacks. So, whether you start a side hustle, invest in stocks, or create online content, you're not only creating revenue streams; you're also paving the route to financial independence and a more resilient future.

- ## 9.1 Exploring Side Hustles and Freelancing.

Have you ever felt like your abilities and interests go beyond your 9-to-5 job? That's where side hustles and freelancing come in - it's like having a job plus something extra on the side. It's not just about making ends meet; it's about doing something you enjoy while earning some additional money.

So, what exactly is a side hustle? Consider it your after-hours passion project. Perhaps you work as a graphic designer during the week and as a weekend photographer to supplement your income. Perhaps you're a teacher who makes handmade jewellery in your spare time. It's about converting your passions or skills into a side hustle without giving up your day job.

Being your boss is similar to freelancing. You can provide you can get paid to offer your abilities, such as writing, graphic design, coding, or even dog walking. Freelancers are the gig economy's modern-day superheroes, taking on jobs from various clients without being tied down to a regular job.

The flexibility of side hustles and freelancing is appealing. You are not bound by a regular work schedule. You are free to work whenever, whenever, and however you want. Do you want to work on an extra project over the weekend or at 2 a.m.? You are capable of doing so. It's about arranging your life around your career, not the other way around.

Let's be honest: it's not all Instagram-worthy coffee shops and flexible schedules. There are difficulties. You must hustle to find clients or customers, manage your own time, and handle company matters.

Invoicing, taxes, and self-promotion all become necessary. It's like you're the CEO, caretaker and creative director of your own small business.

The beauty of side hustles and freelance work is that they frequently begin tiny. You don't need a nice office or a lot of money. You can begin small, see what works, and then expand. It's a path of self-discovery and business in which you determine your success.
And, hey, it's not all about the money - though extra income is always wonderful. It's about doing something you're interested in, learning new skills, and possibly shifting to a career you enjoy. It's a chance to turn "what if" into "I'm doing it."So, whether you're manufacturing homemade soaps, writing articles for clients all over the world, or giving your services on platforms like Upwork or Fiverr, side hustles and freelancing are all about making money. In the workplace, you make your own rules. It's about taking command of your ship, navigating the seas of opportunity, and perhaps discovering a treasure box of fulfilment along the way.

- ## 9.2 Passive Income Strategies

Have you ever wanted to make money while sipping your favourite coffee or watching your favourite TV show? That is the draw of passive income: it is earning without having to constantly clock in and out. So, how can you make your dream a reality? Let's look at some practical passive income strategies.

1. Stock Investing:

- ***Consider stocks to be low-wage employees***. They can provide passive income through dividends if you invest in them. It's like receiving a small bonus from the companies you support simply for being a shareholder.

2. Real Estate Rentals:

Do you have an extra room or a vacant property? You can rent it out. Real estate may be a reliable source of passive income, whether through regular leasing or by getting on the Airbnb bandwagon.

3. Create an Online Course:

If you have a skill or expertise, why not share it with others? Creating an online course allows you to earn money while also educating others. The money keeps coming in once it's up and functioning.

4. Create a book or an ebook:
Have you ever wanted to be an author? Writing, whether it's a paperback or an e-book, can become a source of passive income. Once it's out there, every sale adds to your bottom line with no ongoing effort on your part.

5. Stocks That Pay Dividends:
Dividend-paying equities, like conventional stocks, Take it up a notch, stock. These equities provide a percentage of their profits to shareholders regularly, generating a steady stream of passive income.

6. Affiliate Marketing:
 Have you ever suggested a product to a friend? Affiliate marketing allows you to accomplish this on a larger scale. You promote other people's products and earn a reward when someone purchases through your unique link.

7. Create a Blog or a YouTube Channel:
Turn your hobby into a business by opening a blog or a YouTube channel. Once you've established a loyal following, you can earn money through advertising, sponsorships, or affiliate marketing.

8. Develop a Mobile App:
If you have a great app idea, make it a reality. You can generate money from adverts, in-app purchases, or even selling the program once it's in the app store.

9. Automated Dropshipping:
- Set up an online store without the hassle of managing inventory. With drop shipping, you sell products, and a third party takes care of storage and shipping. Your store runs, and you earn while you sleep. While the idea of passive income is enticing, it's crucial to understand that many of these strategies require upfront effort and time. Building a blog, writing a book, or creating an online course takes dedication. However, once the groundwork is done, the potential for earning without constant active involvement becomes the sweet reward. So, whether you're investing in stocks, renting out a property, or building an online

empire, passive income is about planting seeds today that grow into money trees tomorrow.

- 9.3 Monetizing Hobbies and Talents.

Ever thought about turning what you love doing in your free time into a little money-maker? It's not just a pipe dream – monetizing your hobbies and talents is like adding a dash of financial sweetness to your passion. Let's dive into some real-world ways to make your favourite activities work for your wallet. **

1. Create and Sell Crafts: If you're into crafting, whether it's handmade jewellery, knitwear, or personalized cards, turn it into a business. Etsy and local craft fairs are fantastic platforms to sell your creations and earn a little extra cash.

2. Offer Your Skills as a Service: Got a skill that others might need? Whether it's writing, graphic design, or social media management, platforms like Fiverr or Upwork let you offer your expertise and get paid for it.

3. Start a Blog or YouTube Channel: Love sharing your thoughts, experiences, or how-tos? Start a blog or YouTube channel. Once you build a loyal audience, you can make money through ads, sponsorships, or even selling your products or services.

4. Teach What You Know: If you're an expert in something – be it playing an instrument, speaking a language, or acing a particular subject – offer lessons. You can teach online or even locally, turning your knowledge into a tidy income.

5. Sell Your Photos: If photography is your thing, consider selling your photos online. Platforms like Shutterstock or Adobe Stock allow you to earn money every time someone purchases one of your images.

6. Write a Blog or E-book: Passionate about a certain topic? Share your knowledge by writing a blog or even penning an e-book. Once it's out there, every click or purchase can add to your pocket.

7. Personal Fitness Training: If you enjoy working out, try becoming a personal trainer. You can offer in-person sessions or even create online workout programs. Your passion for staying healthy can become a source of income.

8. Create Online Courses: Turn your skills or expertise into an online course. Platforms like Udemy or Teachable allow you toTeachable allow you to create and sell courses on topics you're passionate about.

9. Streaming Your Gaming Skills: If you're a gamer and enjoy playing video games, consider streaming your gameplay on platforms like Twitch or YouTube Gaming. Making money online can be done through advertisements, donations, and sponsorships.

.10. Offer Your Cooking or Baking Services: Do you love whipping up delicious meals or baking scrumptious treats? Offer your culinary skills to others. You can cater events, sell custom cakes, or even host cooking classes.

11. Rent Your Gear: - If you have high-quality equipment, whether it's a camera, power tools, or camping gear, consider renting it out. Websites like Fat Llama allow you to earn money by lending your equipment to others.

12. Create and Sell Music: - If you're a musician or songwriter, platforms like Spotify, Apple Music, or even SoundCloud provide opportunities to monetize your music. You can also sell your music to fans directly. The key to successfully monetizing your hobbies and talents is finding a balance between passion and practicality. It's about turning what you love into a source of income without losing the joy in it. So, whether you're creating art, teaching, or cooking up a storm, there are real opportunities to turn your hobbies and talents into a side hustle that not only satisfies your passion but also lines your pockets.

Chapter Ten:

Cultivating Generational Wealth.

Have you ever considered leaving a financial legacy for your children, grandchildren, and beyond? That's the allure of building generational wealth: it's like planting a money tree that will continue to grow for future generations. Let's get down to business and figure out how to make this financial fairy tale a reality.

1. Long-Term Investment Planning:

Smart investing is frequently the starting point for generational wealth. The key to investing in stocks, real estate, or other vehicles is to think long-term. Compounding growth over decades can turn little investments into large sums of money.

2. Real Estate as a Foundation: Investing in real estate is similar to creating a solid foundation for future riches. Real estate, whether it is rental property, commercial real estate, or a family residence, has the potential to appreciate over time and offer continual revenue.

3. Trusts and Foundations: Establishing trusts or foundations can be a strategic move. These legal frameworks can protect assets, reduce taxes, and ensure that your money is passed down through generations according to your intentions.

4. Instill Financial Literacy: Knowledge is power. Educating your children and grandchildren on money management, investing, and financial literacy equips them to make good decisions with the wealth that has been passed down to them.

5. enterprising initiatives: Fostering an enterprising spirit within the family can lead to profitable commercial initiatives. Whether it's a family business or supporting individual entrepreneurial endeavours, these activities can help to ensure generational prosperity.

6. Strategic Estate Planning: Proper estate planning ensures that wealth is passed on to the next generation smoothly. This includes wills, trusts, and other mechanisms to reduce estate taxes and guarantee your assets are dispersed by your wishes.

7. Instill a Savings Mindset: It is critical to instil a saving culture within the family. Teaching the value of saving money for future investments, emergencies, or opportunities establishes a financial mindset that lasts generations.

8. Diversify your assets: Don't put all of your financial eggs in one basket. Diversifying assets across multiple investment classes minimises risk while increasing long-term growth potential.

9. Encourage Higher Education: Investing in human capital by supporting education inside the family. Higher education can offer doors to profitable employment, laying the groundwork for future generations to build on.

10. Honest Financial Communication: - Break the silence about money. Open communication about money promotes transparency and guarantees that future generations understand the family's financial goals, values, and methods.

11. Constant Adaptation: As the globe changes, so should your financial plan. Keep up with financial changes, adjust your investment portfolio, and seize new opportunities to guarantee that your generational wealth remains robust.

12. Philanthropy and Social Responsibility: Including philanthropy in your financial strategy can leave a positive legacy. Developing family-giving traditions not only benefits society but also instils values in future generations.

Creating a legacy of financial insight, accountability, and possibilities is what generational wealth is all about. It is a path that requires careful preparation, ongoing education, and the transmission of not only wealth but also the knowledge of how to grow and keep it. So, whether you're investing, educating, or preparing future entrepreneurs, The seeds you plant now in your family can grow into a lasting financial legacy for future generations.

10.1 Wealth Transfer and Estate Planning

Thinking about what happens to your hard-earned possessions when you die may not be the most enjoyable topic, but it is an important element of ensuring your family's financial future. Let's have a serious discussion about estate planning and the art of handing wealth down to the next generation.

1. last will:
Your will is similar to your script for asset distribution. It specifies who receives what, ensuring that your desires are re-followed. It may not be the most fascinating document to write, but it is critical.

2. Trusts: Trusts are the estate planning equivalent of Swiss army knives. They can assist in the effective management and distribution of assets while also providing benefits such as the reduction of estate taxes. There are numerous sorts of trusts, so determining the best fit for your scenario is critical.

3. Power of Attorney: Giving someone you trust power of attorney gives them the authority to make financial choices on your behalf if you are unable to. It serves as a protection to guarantee that your affairs are managed by your intentions.

4. Healthcare Directives: In addition to financial matters, healthcare directives outline your medical treatment preferences if you are unable to communicate. It's a difficult but vital topic to have with your family.
5. Beneficiary Designations: Maintain your beneficiary designations. Whether it's life insurance policies, retirement accounts, or investment accounts, making sure the appropriate people inherit these assets is a critical component of estate planning.

6. Reducing Estate Taxes: While no one enjoys paying taxes, prudent estate planning can assist in reducing them. Gifting, forming trusts, and taking advantage of tax exemptions can all be part of a strategy to lower the tax burden on your inheritance.

7. Periodic Reviews: Life doesn't stop, and neither should your estate plan. Review and revise your plan regularly to reflect changes in your financial status, family dynamics, or even changes in the law.

8. Open Family Conversations: Discussing money and inheritance can be difficult, but open conversations with your family can help avoid misunderstandings and ensure everyone is on the same page. Discussing your desires can help you avoid future disagreements.

9. particular Circumstances: If you have family members who have particular needs or are in unusual circumstances, your estate plan should be tailored to their individual needs. This could include establishing trusts or naming guardians.

10. Professional Advice: - Estate planning is not a one-size-fits-all proposition. Seeking professional guidance, such as from estate attorneys and financial planners, can assist in tailoring a strategy that corresponds with your goals and ensuring all legalities are covered.

11. Charitable Giving: If philanthropy is important to you, include charitable giving in your estate plan. Donating to causes that are important to you can have a long-term influence.

12. Important Documents Organisation: - Organise vital paperwork to make life easy for your loved ones. Having everything in one location, from your will and trust paperwork to financial account details, ensures a smoother process for your heirs.

Remember, estate planning isn't only about the "what ifs"; it's about taking control of your financial legacy and safeguarding the well-being of your loved ones. While it may entail some difficult discussions and paperwork, it is ultimately an act of love and duty that spans generations. So, whether you're writing your will, updating beneficiaries, or planning a trip, By discussing your estate plan with your family, you're building the framework for a smoother wealth transfer and the protection of your financial legacy.

Teaching financial literacy

Teaching financial literacy to your family may not be as simple as teaching arithmetic problems, but it is an important skill that will set everyone up for a lifetime of financial well-being. Let's talk about some practical methods to make financial education a family affair.

1. **Regular Family Money Talks**: Instead of avoiding the subject of money, make it a regular family event. Discussing budgets, spending, and financial goals openly fosters an environment in which everyone can learn and participate.

2. **Lessons for Different Age Groups:** Tailor your lessons to different age groups. For the younger ones, it may be as easy as grasping the notion of saving, whilst teenagers may be ready for discussions about budgeting and credit management.

3. **Budgeting Experiments**: Make budgeting a hands-on experience. Set aside time as a family to build a budget. Assign responsibilities, track spending, and determine where changes can be made. It's a useful financial decision-making lesson.

4. **Saving Jars for objectives**: Introduce the notion of saving for objectives through the use of jars. One for short-term goals, such as a family outing, and another for long-term ones, such as a vacation. It illustrates the significance of setting money away for various needs.

5. **Involve the Family in Financial Decisions**: Involve the family in financial decisions, whether it's picking on a vacation destination or deciding on family spending. It teaches not only financial decision-making but also the importance of everyone's contribution.

6. **Make Use of Real-Life Examples:**

Connect financial ideas to real-world examples. Connecting theory to reality makes it more approachable, whether it's comparing supermarket prices, explaining interest rates with a loan example, or addressing the family's monthly bills.

7. Savings Matching: To encourage savings, offer to match a percentage of what each family member saves. It encourages everyone to contribute to savings objectives and emphasises the concept of "free money" through matching donations.

8. Board Games with Financial Lessons: Board games such as Monopoly or The Game of Life teach valuable lessons in budgeting, investing, and dealing with unforeseen financial issues. Make family game night into a lesson in financial literacy.

9. Teach the Fundamentals of Investment: As the family expands, teach the fundamentals of investment. Discuss various investing alternatives, how they function, and the possibility of long-term growth. It lays the framework for comprehending the role of investment in wealth creation.

10. Share Your Personal Financial Experiences: - Discuss your own financial experiences, both achievements and failures. It's a method to humanise financial concepts and demonstrate that everyone, especially grownups, is still learning and growing along the road.

11. Foster an Entreprencurial Spirit: - Encourage an entrepreneurial spirit in the family. It promotes the value of initiative, creativity, and financial independence, whether it's starting a modest family business or fostering individual activities.

12. Mark Financial Milestones: - Family financial milestones should be celebrated. Recognising accomplishments, whether it's paying off a debt, hitting a savings goal, or effectively budgeting for a family trip, encourages excellent financial habits.

Remember that teaching financial literacy is a continuous conversation and learning process, not a one-time lecture. Making it a family affair allows you to not only transmit financial knowledge but also to foster a supportive environment in which everyone can grow and make informed financial decisions. So, whether you're talking about budgets, playing financial games, or sharing personal experiences, every moment counts. Every hour counts towards creating a financially savvy and powerful household.

30-Day Money Makeover: Simple Steps to Financial Freedom"

Day 1: Know What Rich Means to You
Day 2: Track Your Spending
Day 3: Set a Money Goal
Day 4: Learn a Money Skill
Day 5: Spend Mindfully
Day 6: Make a Basic Budget
Day 7: Start a Daily Money Habit
Day 8: Explore Simple Investments
Day 9: Reflect on Your Money Feelings
Day 10: Share Money Tips with a Friend
Day 11: Find and Cut Unneeded Spending
Day 12: Plan a Side Gig
Day 13: Check Out Easy Money Resources
Day 14: Write Your Money Goals
Day 15: Connect with Money-Smart Friends
Day 16: Track Your Daily Spending
Day 17: Read a Simple Money Book
Day 18: Begin an Emergency Fund
Day 19: Look into Easy Investments
Day 20: Think Savings
Day 21: Check Your Money Health
Day 22: Be Thankful for Your Money
Day 23: Plan for Paying Off Debts
Day 24: Take a Free Money Class Online
Day 25: Create a Simple Investment Plan
Day 26: Picture Your Money Goals
Day 27: Ask for Discounts
Day 28: Review Your Progress
Day 29: Chat with Money Pros
Day 30: Celebrate Your Money Wins and Plan for More.